W9-BYO-094

Touch the Earth

by **Jane Baskwill**
illustrations by **Peter Fiore**

Text copyright © 1999 by Jane Baskwill
Illustrations copyright © 1999 by Peter Fiore

All rights reserved.
No part of this publication may be reproduced, except in the case of quotation
for articles or reviews, or stored in any retrieval system, or transmitted in any form
or by any means, electronic, mechanical, photocopying, recording, or otherwise,
without written permission from the publisher.
For information contact:
MONDO Publishing
980 Avenue of the Americas
New York, NY 10018
MONDO is a registered trademark of Mondo Publishing
Visit our website at http://www.mondopub.com

Printed in China
06 07 08   9 8 7 6 5

Book design by Edward Miller

Library of Congress Cataloging-in-Publication Data
Baskwill, Jane.
Touch the earth / by Jane Baskwill ; illustrated by Peter Fiore.
p.   cm.
ISBN 1-57255-428-2 (pbk. : alk. paper)
[1. Nature—Fiction.]   I. Fiore, Peter M., ill.   II. Title.
PZ7.B29235To   1998
[E]—dc21   97-3944
CIP
AC

For Geoffrey, the eldest, and Amanda-Lynn,
the youngest—J.B.

For my Lisa and Paul—P.F.

The Earth touches you in many ways . . .
in the way a warm spring rain washes your face,

in the way a dandelion seed tickles your nose,

in the way a gentle breeze combs your hair.

The Earth touches you in many ways . . .
in the way a cricket's summer lullaby sings you to sleep,

in the way a field of daisies invites you to play,

in the way the wind seems to call your name.

The Earth touches you in many ways . . .
in the way colorful gardens give you food,

in the way cool winding streams give you water,

in the way leaf-laden trees give you shelter.

The Earth touches you in many ways.
And you can touch the Earth, too.

Touch the Earth with your kindness . . .
when you feed the birds,

when you create a butterfly garden,

when you plant a tree.

HELP
US
ADOPT
AN
ANIMAL

Touch the Earth with your thoughtfulness . . .
when you adopt an endangered animal,

when you save an acre of rain forest,

when you go on a beach sweep.

Touch the Earth with your happiness . . .
when you sing songs,

when you share stories,

when you draw pictures.

When you touch the Earth,
you show you care.

Would you like to "touch the Earth"?

There are many things you can do to help the Earth. Some are very simple things you can do by yourself or with friends or classmates. Others take more time and planning, and you may need the help of an adult.

Here is a list of books with ideas for things you can do. Look for these books in bookstores and libraries.

The Big Book of Nature Projects by The Children's School of Science. Thames and Hudson, New York, NY, 1997.

Earth Book for Kids by Linda Schwartz. Learning Works, Santa Barbara, CA, 1990.

The Jumbo Book of Nature Science by Pamela Hickman and The Federation of Ontario Naturalists. Kids Can Press, Toronto, Canada, 1996.

The Little Hands Nature Book by Nancy Fusco Castaldo. Williamson Publishing, Charlotte, VT, 1997.

More Teaching Kids to Love the Earth by James Kasperson and Marina Lachecki. Pfeifer-Hamilton, Duluth, MN, 1994.

Play and Find Out About Nature: Easy Experiments for Young Children by Janice Pratt VanCleave. John Wiley and Sons, New York, NY, 1997.

Projects for a Healthy Planet by Shar Levine and Allison Grafton. John Wiley and Sons, New York, NY, 1992.

Take Action: An Environmental Book for Kids by Ann Love and Jane Drake. Kids Can Press, Toronto, Canada, 1993.

Teaching Kids to Love the Earth by Marina Lachecki Herman, Joseph Passineau, Ann Schimpf, and Paul Treuer. Pfeifer-Hamilton, Duluth, MN, 1990.